Dungeness Crab

Embarcadero– "Eclipse"

49-Mile Drive

In-line Skating

Japantown

North Beach

Octagon House

Point Reyes

Sourdough Bread

T'ai Chi

Cable Car X-ing

Yerba Buena

Zschock

Martha Schock

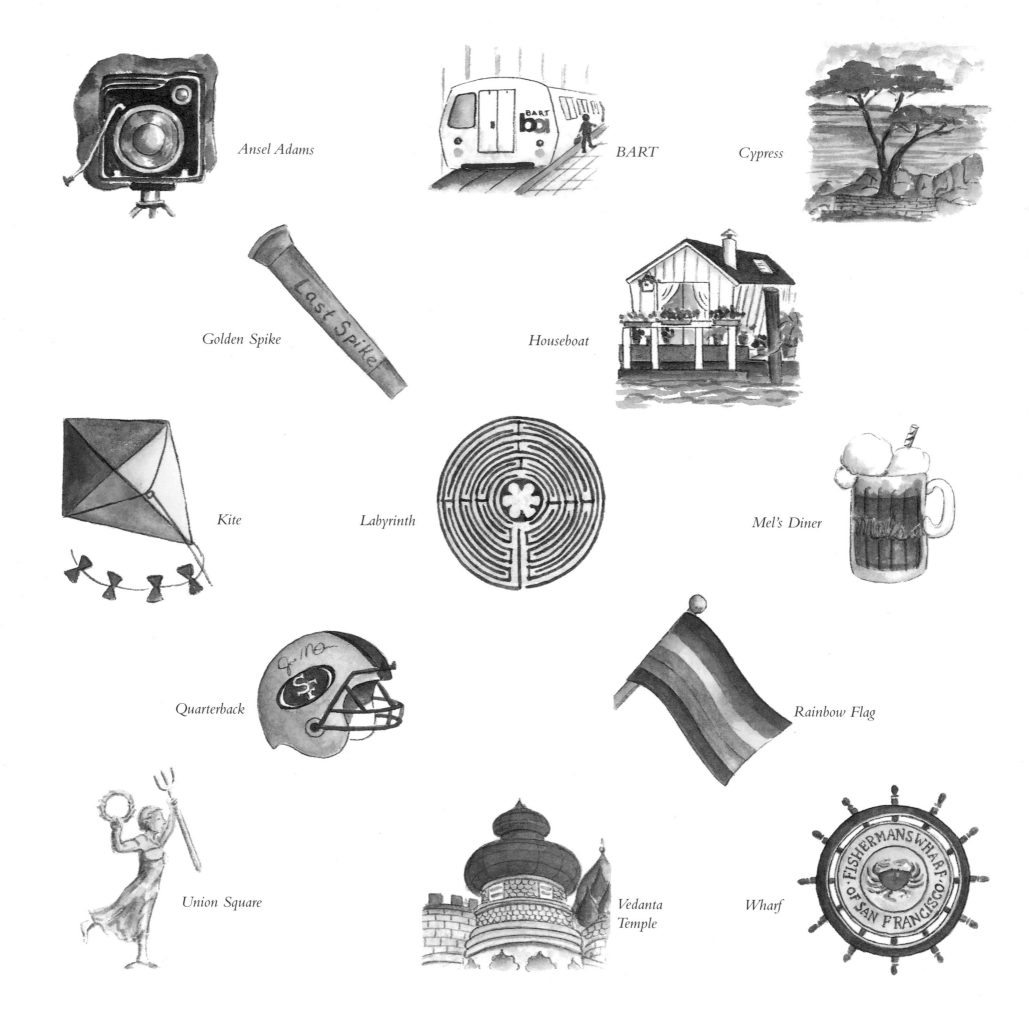

Ansel Adams

BART

Cypress

Golden Spike

Houseboat

Kite

Labyrinth

Mel's Diner

Quarterback

Rainbow Flag

Union Square

Vedanta Temple

Wharf

Journey Around

San Francisco
from A to Z

Martha Day Zschock

COMMONWEALTH EDITIONS

Beverly, Massachusetts

Bon Voyage Michelle !
Love, Avery

Commonwealth Editions
An imprint of Memoirs Unlimited, Inc.
266 Cabot Street
Beverly, Massachusetts 01915
Visit Commonwealth Editions at www.commonwealtheditions.com

Visit Martha Zschock at www.journeyaround.com

ISBN 1-889833-49-5

10 9 8 7 6 5 4 3 2 1

Printed in Korea

To my wonderful family

and to all those who follow
their golden dreams
despite the ups and downs
of the journey

A special thank-you to those who have helped with this journey around San Francisco, including Emily Britton,
Br. Guire Cleary at Mission Dolores, Denise and Bill Shields and Ratz at the Artists Inn, Dr. Robert Chandler at the Wells Fargo Bank,
Judy DeBella at the San Francisco Museum and Historical Society, and Craig Glassner at the Golden Gate National Recreation Area.

I left my heart . . .

in San Francisco

Greetings, my friends, and
Welcome to San Francisco!

THE BEAUTIFUL, HILLY CITY OF SAN FRANCISCO sits atop a peninsula, with the Pacific Ocean to the west and the rest of the country to the east across the bay. The city has a past as colorful as its famous houses known as "Painted Ladies," and a future where anything is imaginable.

The area remained undiscovered by European settlers until about 150 years after the Pilgrims landed in Plymouth, Massachusetts. When gold was discovered in the Sierra Nevada Foothills in 1848, a boom began and waves of people flooded to the region; dreamers from all over the globe came anticipating instant wealth, while entrepreneurs and laborers saw a golden opportunity.

For a city so young, San Francisco has shown great determination and resiliency. In this short time, it has suffered three devastating earthquakes and a major fire. Like the ups and downs of San Francisco's steep streets, the city reaches higher and higher each time it rebuilds. Offering a ready welcome to people of all colors and creeds, San Francisco has become one of the most diverse and culturally rich cities on earth.

Come, there's much to explore. Let's take a journey around San Francisco!

All around town, hills abound.

VanNess Ave. California
59
& Market Streets

BEFORE THE INVENTION OF THE CABLE CAR IN 1873, few lived on San Francisco's steep hills. After Andrew Hallidie witnessed a horse-drawn tram slipping down an incline, he was determined to find a better way to carry people up the slopes. His invention of the cable car was so successful that by the 1880s property values along the eight cable car lines multiplied. Today, the beloved cable cars are a National Historic Landmark.

To move forward, cable cars grip a continually moving cable. A skilled brake person and conductor work together to operate the cars.

Cable car, Nob Hill
Inset: Lombard Street, North Beach
Detail: Cable Car Museum, Nob Hill

Beautiful blossoms blow in bay breezes.

FORMS OF DAHLIA

Collerette

Cactus

Ball

Decorative

AS SAN FRANCISCO QUICKLY GREW FROM A SMALL PORT TO A MAJOR CITY, its citizens wanted what other large cities had, a park with open space and greenery. William Hall and John McLaren transformed the sandy, windswept area west of the city into a serene natural setting known today as Golden Gate Park. They selected thousands of botanical varieties to ensure continuous blossoms throughout the year.

Conservatory of Flowers, Golden Gate Park
Inset: Dahlia Garden, Golden Gate Park
Detail: Stow Lake, Golden Gate Park

Gently paddling along Stow Lake is a serene alternative to the hustle and bustle of city life.

Chinese culture contributes character to the city.

HARD-WORKING CHINESE IMMIGRANTS contributed greatly to the development of California and San Francisco. Despite low wages, they worked tirelessly in gold mines, helped build railroads, and planted vineyards. Their strong community prevailed in the face of many challenges, and Chinese-Americans now enjoy the freedoms of the country they helped to build.

Fortune cookies, often served following a meal in a Chinese restaurant, are actually a Japanese invention! They were first created in Golden Gate Park's Japanese Tea Garden in 1909.

Bank of Canton, Chinatown
Inset: Chinese New Year celebration
Detail: Golden Gate Fortune Cookies, Chinatown

Diggers dreamed of discovering gold.

WELLS FARGO & CO. OVERLAND STAGE

U.S. MAIL

Lake Superior

Lake Michigan

Lake Huron

Sacramento

San Francisco

Pacific Ocean

St. Joseph

Gulf of Mexico

Key
— Central Route
— Ox Bow-or-"Butterfield Route
— Other Routes

IN 1848, JAMES MARSHALL discovered gold in the Sierra Foothills. He excitedly shared his find with his boss, John Sutter, and the two men vowed to keep it a secret. The secret didn't last long. By 1849, the race for gold was on. San Francisco's population skyrocketed to 20,000 within the year. Wells, Fargo & Company soon ran expresses to and from the region. Today, Wells Fargo is one of the world's leading banks.

Stagecoach, Wells Fargo History Museum
Inset: Miners
Details: Covered wagon and abandoned ships

In their rush to the gold mines, "49ers" abandoned their ships in the bay.
Others arrived in covered wagons after a long, bumpy, dangerous ride.

Entre-
Epreneurs
established
leading
enterprises.

AFTER SAM BRENNAN STOCKED HIS STORE WITH MINING EQUIPMENT, he announced, "Gold! Gold! Gold from the American River!" to the people of San Francisco. This spurred on the gold rush and, with it, an entrepreneurial spirit. Businesses serving the newly wealthy miners provided such goods as chocolate (Ghirardelli), bread (Boudin Bakery), and coffee (Folgers). Levi Strauss realized that tent fabric could also make durable trousers—and launched the company we know as Levi's.

The Pony Express became famous for its speedy, reliable mail service between St. Joseph, Missouri, and San Francisco.

Ghirardelli Square
Inset: Levi's Plaza, North Beach
Detail: Pony Express rider

Fog floats in frequently.

MARK TWAIN REPORTEDLY STATED, "The coldest winter I ever spent was a summer in San Francisco." Like most good jokes, this one has the ring of truth. Summer days can be chilly, damp, and foggy. The city's famous fog gives it a mysterious romance—and eventually gives way to the bright sunshine of September and October. The temperature rarely drops below 40°F, and anything over 80°F is considered a heat wave!

Fog City Diner, North Beach
Inset: Sutro Tower, West of Mission
Detail: Fog signal building and lighthouse, Alcatraz

To help boats navigate, each foghorn has its own unique blast and each lighthouse flashes a different pattern.

FOR OVER TWO CENTURIES European explorers sailed past the Golden Gate, the narrow entrance to San Francisco's magnificent bay. After its discovery in 1769, it was seen as an important strategic location. In 1860, Fort Point was built at the Presidio on the site of an old Spanish battery. Today the majestic Golden Gate Bridge spans the entrance to the bay, and visitors can view the area's military past throughout the Golden Gate National Recreation Area.

About fifty painters work year-round to maintain the bridge, America's most photographed structure. It is painted "international orange" to stand out in fog.

Golden Gate Bridge
Inset: Red Brick Barracks, Presidio
Detail: Brave bridge painter

Hippies hung out in the Haight.

PEACE

Happiness

LOVE

PEACE LOVE

FLOWER POWER

HAIGHT ASHBURY

WHEN THE DEPRESSION OF THE 1930s HIT THE HAIGHT-ASHBURY NEIGHBORHOOD, many of its upper-class Victorian homes were divided into inexpensive apartments and fell into disrepair. Low rents attracted the "beats" of the 1950s and the "hippies" of the 1960s. Although this peace-loving generation is remembered for its love of rock 'n' roll and its use of illegal drugs, it left a legacy of social tolerance and acceptance.

Corner of Haight and Ashbury Streets
Inset: Hippie attire
Detail: Cherry Garcia—yum!

The Grateful Dead was a rock 'n' roll band that got its start in San Francisco in the 1960s. Ben & Jerry's "Cherry Garcia" ice cream pays tribute to the band's leader, Jerry Garcia.

I solated Alcatraz imprisoned infamous inmates.

NAMED ISLA DE LOS ALCATRACES (ISLAND OF THE PELICANS) by Spanish settlers, Alcatraz was the site of the first U.S. fort on the West Coast. From 1934 to 1963, the island housed a maximum-security prison. The prison closed when the government determined that the cost of keeping prisoners on "The Rock" equaled that of the finest hotels. Today, Alcatraz is a national park, where native grasses and flowers are flourishing once again.

From 1969 to 1971, Indians of All Tribes occupied Alcatraz, an event that brought attention to the rights of Native Americans.

Alcatraz
Inset: Cell block, Alcatraz
Detail: Native American occupation

Junks and feluccas journeyed from jetties.

BEFORE TRAINS, PLANES, AND AUTOMOBILES, San Francisco was accessible primarily by water, as the overland journey by covered wagon or stagecoach was long and dangerous. As a result, the city became an important international port. Waterways bustled with ships from the four corners of the earth, and ferryboats shuttled passengers across the bay. The opening of the Golden Gate and Bay Bridges made travel to and from San Francisco even easier.

Hyde Street Pier
Inset: Ferry Building, Financial District
Details: Chinese junk (left) and Italian felucca (right)

Immigrants built fishing boats like those in their native countries. Italians fished from feluccas and Chinese sailed junks.

K ids in the know, know just where to go!

Bubbles at the Exploratorium

Starfish at the California Academy of Sciences

Carousel at Yerba Buena Gardens

SAN FRANCISCO HAS PLENTY OF FUN PLACES TO LEARN NEW THINGS. Visitors can travel land, sea, and space at the California Academy of Sciences; explore the five senses at the Exploratorium; learn by playing at the Bay Area Discovery Museum; walk through history at the Oakland Museum of California; or become a chemist at the Lawrence Hall of Science. Wherever families go, learning is fun.

Thanks to the San Francisco Recreation and Park Department, the city boasts fifty-two playgrounds for children.

"Puddle Jumpers," Transamerica Redwood Park
Inset: Fun places to go
Detail: Playground, Chinatown

Loving labor leaves a lasting legacy.

REMEMBERING LOVED ONES LOST TO A DEADLY DISEASE, family and friends from around the globe have joined to create the AIDS Memorial Quilt. Called the Names Project, the quilt is made up of thousands of three-by-six-foot panels. It is the largest community art project in the world. Several panels figured prominently in President Clinton's 1993 inaugural parade.

Grace Cathedral, Nob Hill
Inset: Volunteer sewing AIDS Quilt
Detail: AIDS Memorial Grove, Golden Gate Park

The National AIDS Memorial Grove honors those lost to this tragic disease.
It is a place for family and friends to remember, to heal, and to hope.

Many
marvel
at the Mission's
murals.

MANY OF SAN FRANCISCO'S COLORFUL MURALS can be seen in the Mission District. They depict themes from the city's present and past, reflecting its diverse cultures. At the heart of the district sits the oldest building in San Francisco, Mission Dolores, established by Spaniards to convert Native Americans to Christianity. Its museum houses Guillermo Granizo's poignant tile mural honoring the native peoples of the region.

A series of murals about California's workers and resources, created during the 1930s, are displayed in Coit Tower.

Cesar Chavez School, Mission District
Inset: Mission Dolores, Mission District
Detail: Coit Tower, North Beach

Nature's noble splendor nurtures the spirit.

BECAUSE THEY WERE DIFFICULT TO REACH, the redwood forests north of San Francisco were spared the fate of most northern California forests: they weren't cut down by loggers. Many trees here are over 200 feet tall and 500 years old! This awe-inspiring forest was named Muir Woods in honor of the great naturalist John Muir, whose teachings about the environment still inspire us to protect our natural treasures.

Redwood trees, Muir Woods
Inset: Monarch butterflies, Muir Beach
Detail: Gray whales, Gulf of the Farallones National Marine Sanctuary

Creatures great and small—California gray whales and monarch butterflies—migrate along the coast of northern California.

Ornate opulence surrounds city hall.

CITY HALL, the centerpiece of San Francisco's grand Beaux Arts Civic Center, has a dome higher than the U.S. Capitol in Washington, D.C. The vibrant area surrounding city hall also includes an opera house and symphony hall, the main branch of the San Francisco Public Library, a veterans' building, and UN Plaza.

Located near the Civic Center, quaint Cottage Row was saved from disrepair by a restoration grant.

City Hall, Civic Center
Inset: *Swan Lake*, War Memorial Opera House
Detail: Cottage Row, Pacific Heights

Painted Ladies portray a proud past.

Italianate style

Queen Anne style

Eastlake style

ORNATE VICTORIAN HOUSES were modern when they were built in the late 1800s, partly because of their indoor plumbing. Many burned in the fire following San Francisco's 1906 earthquake, and others were torn down by later generations who viewed them as monstrosities. Originally painted in subtle shades, they were repainted with bright colors in the 1970s. Nicknamed "Painted Ladies," many are being lovingly restored to their original splendor.

Painted Ladies, Alamo Square
Inset: Styles of Victorian houses
Detail: Bay window, Pacific Heights

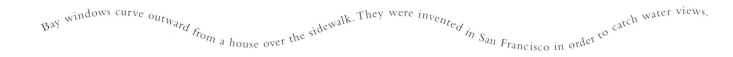
Bay windows curve outward from a house over the sidewalk. They were invented in San Francisco in order to catch water views.

Quivering quakes led to quality architecture.

IN 1906 AND 1989, San Francisco suffered two major earthquakes, the result of shifting tectonic plates beneath the earth's surface. Aware of the damage earthquakes can cause, Californians have developed remarkably strong and stable buildings to withstand the strongest vibrations. The Transamerica Pyramid is designed to move with tremors in the earth, while many older buildings are undergoing "seismic retrofitting" to make them safe.

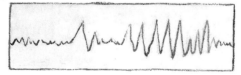

Scientists study the intensity of an earthquake by reading the printout from a seismograph.

Transamerica Pyramid, Financial District
Inset: SafeQuake, California Academy of Sciences, Golden Gate Park
Detail: Seismograph printout

Racial diversity enriches the region.

No, No, we are not satisfied, and we will not be satisfied until justice rolls down like water and righteousness like a mighty stream.

Martin Luther King, Jr.
Washington, D.C. 1963

WHILE IMMIGRANT GROUPS have not always felt welcome, most now find San Francisco a remarkably tolerant and open community. Monuments in the city recall the struggle for equality while honoring the richness provided by racial diversity. Martin Luther King Jr., who is memorialized in Yerba Buena Gardens, was one of those who worked tirelessly to promote equality and freedom for everyone.

Today a Miwok village in Marin County recalls a time, before Spanish settlement, when Indians lived peacefully in the Bay Area.

Moon Bridge, Japanese Tea Garden
Inset: Martin Luther King Jr. Memorial
Detail: (left) Tule reed hut, Mission Dolores, (right) bark hut, Kule Loklo Village, Point Reyes National Seashore

Spectators snap photos of sunbathing sea lions.

PIER 39

HARRASSMENT OF SEA LIONS IS A VIOLATION OF THE MARINE MAMMAL PROTECTION ACT

MARINE BIOLOGISTS WERE BAFFLED when a large group of sea lions made Pier 39 their home following the 1989 earthquake. Local merchants feared the animals' loud barking would discourage business, but tourists love them! The Bay Model, a two-acre indoor re-creation of San Francisco Bay, allowed scientists to study the effects of human activity on the natural environment of the bay.

Adolph Sutro helped protect California's seals by keeping hunters away from Seal Rocks, just offshore from his Cliff House.

Pier 39 at Fisherman's Wharf
Inset: Bay Model Visitor Center, Sausalito
Detail: Cliff House and Seal Rocks, west of Golden Gate Park

Telegraph's tower tops the town.

THE SEVERITY OF THE 1906 EARTHQUAKE was slight compared with the devastating fire it caused. Broken water mains made fighting the fire nearly impossible. The blaze finally was brought under control after three days, when winds shifted and rain appeared. Coit Tower, a tribute to the city's firefighters, was built with funds left by Lillie Hitchcock Coit. As a child, she so loved the firefighters that the Knickerbocker Fire Company made her an honorary member.

Coit Tower, Telegraph Hill
Inset: San Francisco Fire Dept. Museum
Detail: Golden Hydrant, Mission District

In the 1906 fire, one working hydrant miraculously saved the heart of the Mission District. Each year that hydrant gets a coat of gold paint.

Universities foster understanding.

STUDENTS FROM AROUND THE WORLD aspire to attend universities in the Bay Area. Stanford, in Palo Alto, is one of the country's most prestigious private universities. The University of California at Berkeley boasts more Nobel laureates than any other in the United States. One of the schools of higher learning in San Francisco proper is the University of California at San Francisco, which is noted for its graduate programs in health sciences.

Founded by Jesuits in 1855, the University of San Francisco is now coeducational and nondenominational.

Memorial Church, Stanford University
Inset: Sather Tower, Berkeley
Details: Hard-working university students

Various sports invite viewers and adventurers.

San Francisco's moderate climate and proximity to the water make it a perfect city for athletes who love the great outdoors. From daredevil hang-gliders to in-line skaters, from surfers catching waves beneath the Golden Gate Bridge to triathletes "escaping from Alcatraz," adventurers are everywhere. PacBell Park is the beautiful waterfront home of the San Francisco Giants baseball team, while Candlestick Park hosts the San Francisco 49ers football team.

Hang-glider, Fort Funston
Inset: Giants slugger
Detail: Trained water spaniel, PacBell Park

When a home run ball from PacBell Park splashes into McCovey Cove, water spaniels race kayakers to retrieve the souvenir.

Workers harvest a wealth of resources.

FISH
CRABS
SHRIMP
LOBSTE

YUM!

HOT CLAM CHOWDER

...ISH

CRABS

THE COUNTRYSIDE AROUND SAN FRANCISCO has provided everything from gold, coal, and oil to rich soil for growing crops and raising animals. Farmers produce a bounty that includes oranges, nuts, grapes, and tomatoes. Offshore waters offer abundant fish and shell-fish. In the past, some methods of farming have hurt the environment. Today, new organic methods are being used to raise crops throughout the region.

PELICAN BRAND

In years past, citrus growers designed eye-catching labels for their fruit crates. Today these labels are collector's items.

Grapes, Napa Valley
Inset: Fresh crabs, Fisherman's Wharf
Detail: Orange crate

E**X**po exalted
the rising
phoenix.

Palace of Fine Arts, Marina District
Inset: Tower of Jewels
Detail: Phoenix

SAN FRANCISCO CELEBRATED ITS RECOVERY from the 1906 earthquake and fire by hosting the Panama-Pacific International Exposition in 1915. The crowning glory of the fair was the dazzling Tower of Jewels. Author Laura Ingalls Wilder visited the extravaganza with her daughter, Rose. Her letters describing its grandeur were later published in a book, *West from Home*. The Palace of Fine Arts, rebuilt since that time, is the only remnant of this remarkable Expo.

San Francisco's recovery after 1906 is often compared with the phoenix, a mythical bird reborn from the ashes of a great fire. It's no wonder the city seal includes a phoenix.

Young Yerba Buena yielded today's city.

Key
☐ Then
☐ Now

SPANIARDS WHO FIRST SETTLED THE AREA built a sleepy village they called Yerba Buena. Renamed San Francisco in 1847, the city has changed in many other ways. Much of today's waterfront was created by filling in the peninsula's coastline. In the late 1900s, a rebuilding project brought new life to an area south of Market Street. Yerba Buena Gardens became the serene centerpiece of San Francisco's cultural life, reflecting the city's commitment to the needs of its citizens.

Yerba Buena (Spanish for "good herb") is the name of a sweet mint that Spanish settlers found growing abundantly on nearby hills and dunes.

Yerba Buena Gardens
Inset: Waterfront then and now
Detail: Yerba Buena mint

Zephyr **Z**ebra train zips through the zoo.

AT THE SAN FRANCISCO ZOO, a speedy train offers visitors a view of over 1,000 species of animals. The zoo includes Gorilla World (one of the world's largest exhibits of animals in their natural habitat), Lorikeet Landing, and Koala Crossing. The new lemur exhibit houses many species of these unusual primates native to Madagascar. Visitors can help feed the lemurs from special activity towers.

Lion exhibit, San Francisco Zoo
Inset: Lipman Family Lemur Forest
Detail: Children's Zoo

The Children's Zoo allows kids to pet, feed, and even brush some of the animals.

Dungeness Crab

Embarcadero—
"Eclipse"

49-Mile Drive

In-line Skating

Japantown

North Beach

Octagon
House

Point
Reyes

Sourdough Bread

T'ai Chi

Cable Car
X-ing

Yerba Buena

Zschock

Martha
Schock

Ansel Adams

BART

Cypress

Golden Spike

Houseboat

Kite

Labyrinth

Mel's Diner

Quarterback

Rainbow Flag

Union Square

Vedanta Temple

Wharf